BE A SMART SHOPPER

Messner Books by Kathlyn Gay

BE A SMART SHOPPER
THE GERMANS HELPED BUILD AMERICA
CAREERS IN SOCIAL SERVICE
BETH DONNIS: SPEECH THERAPIST
GIRL PILOT

Elm Road Library
P-H-M School Corporation
Mishawaka, Indiana

BE A SMART SHOPPER

by Kathlyn Gay

Photographs by
David C. Sassman

Julian Messner   New York

Published by Julian Messner, a Division of Simon & Schuster, Inc.
1 West 39 Street, New York, N.Y. 10018. All rights reserved.

Text Copyright © 1974 by Kathlyn Gay
Photographs copyright © 1974 by David C. Sassman

Printed in the United States of America

Design by Madeline Bastis

Library of Congress Cataloging in Publication Data

Gay, Kathlyn.
Be a smart shopper.

SUMMARY: Explains advertising psychology, comparative shopping, and consumer protection and advises the reader in being a more responsible shopper.
1. Consumer education—Juvenile literature.
[1. Consumer education] I. Sassman, David C., illus. II. Title.
TX335.G39   640.73   74-7593
ISBN 0-671-32695-3
ISBN 0-671-32696-1 (lib. bdg.)

We appreciate being able to use the facilities of the following businesses for photographic purposes: Mr. Friendly Pet Shop, The Book Shack, Kar Kare Corner, The Toy Soldier, The Butcher Block and Thrifty Mart in South Bend, Indiana; also, Newman's Pharmacy, Wilt's Food Center, Cook's Discount Store, and G.L. Perry Variety Store in Elkhart, Indiana. We are especially grateful for the help of Big Brothers and Big Sisters organizations of St. Joseph County (South Bend, Indiana).

K.G. and D.S.

CONTENTS

Chapter

One	**Who Is A Consumer?**	9
Two	**Where You Can Buy**	16
Three	**Why You Buy**	25
Four	**Beware of Ballyhoo!**	31
Five	**What's The Best Buy?**	39
Six	**How Is A Consumer Protected?**	49
	Index	63

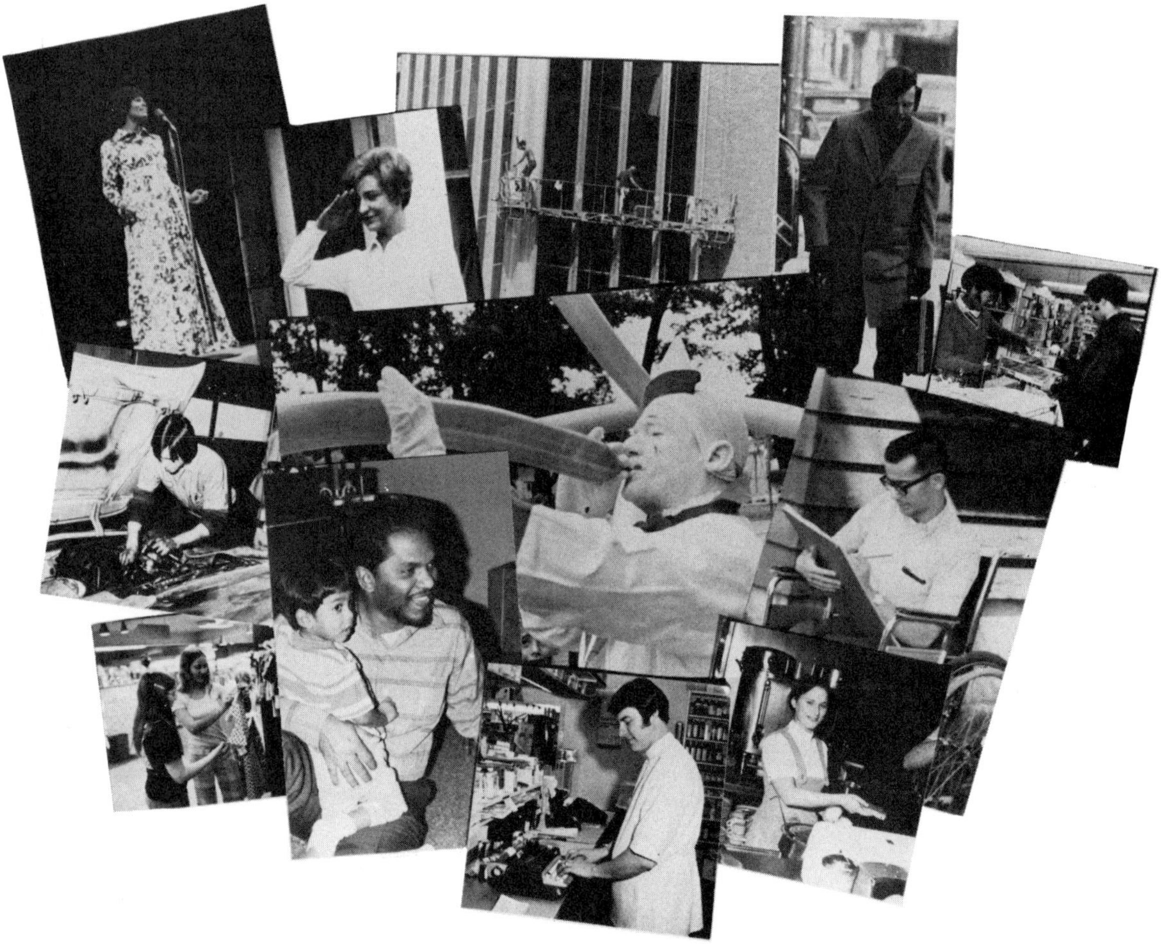

CHAPTER ONE

WHO IS A CONSUMER?

Young or old, rich or poor, tall or short—millions of people live in this country. They live on farms, in cities, in suburbs. They work at many different jobs. They have different religions and come from different backgrounds. They have different likes and dislikes.

Yet, all these people have one thing in common. They are *consumers.* They use *goods,* such as shoes, cars, and paint, and *services* like medical care and the telephone. Any time a person uses up goods and services, that person is consuming or being a consumer.

In order to survive, every person consumes certain goods and services such as food, clothing, and shelter. These are called *necessities.* When goods and services make life easier or more comfortable, they are called *luxuries* or conveniences. People consume luxury items just because they like or want to have them.

In some cases, though, what is a necessity for one person can be a luxury for another. Suppose you get a bicycle in order to keep up a newspaper route or to make deliveries for a neighborhood store. You need the bike for your job, so it is a necessity. On the other hand, another boy or girl might want a new ten-

For survival, every person needs food and other goods often purchased in large supermarkets.

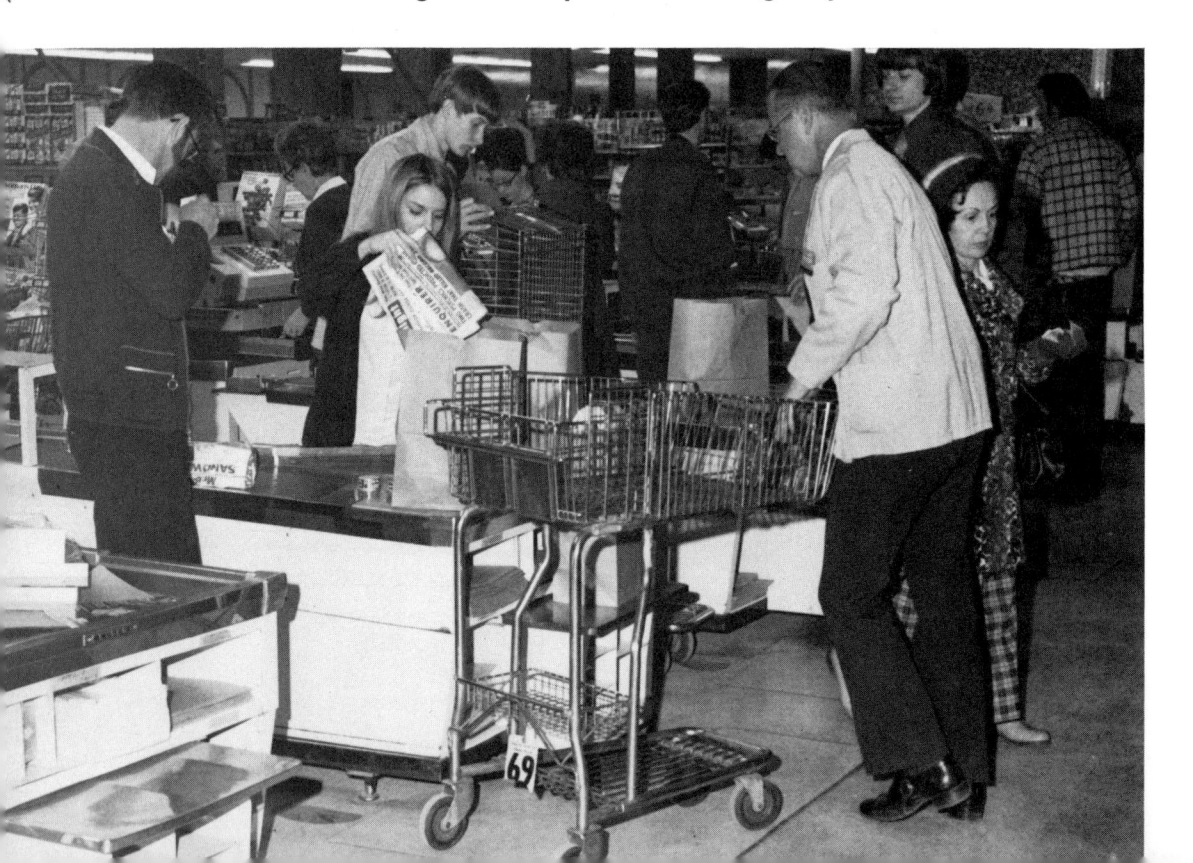

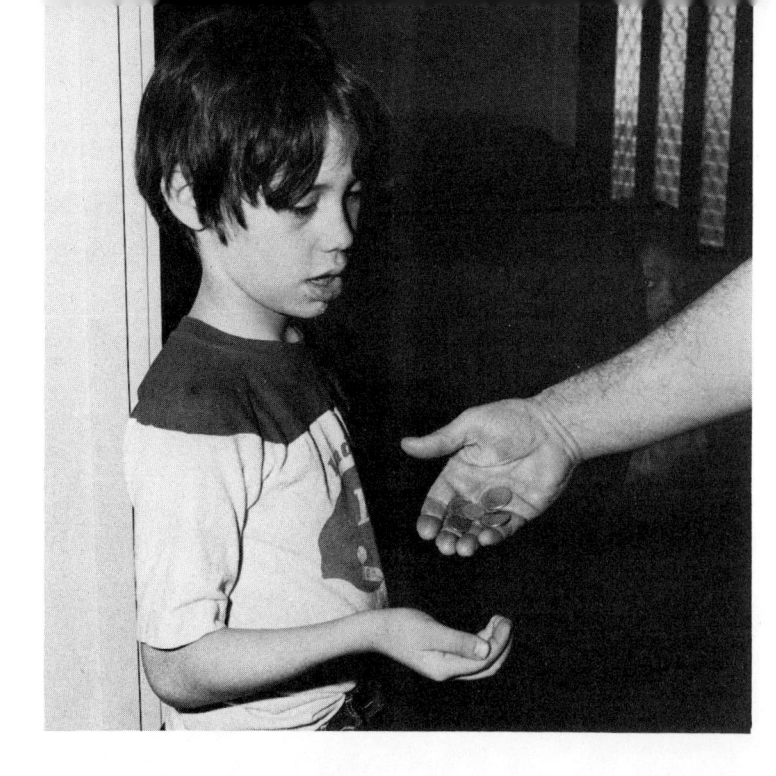

In order to buy the goods and services you need, you might earn money by doing chores around the house or by mowing lawns or doing errands.

speed bicycle just because it's fun to have one. Then the bike would be a luxury.

To pay for goods and services, most of us must have *income.* This is usually money earned from a job. Young people often earn money by mowing lawns, cleaning yards, baby-sitting, or doing errands. Sometimes an allowance is paid for chores done around the house.

Rewards and prizes of value, instead of money, can also be earned. For example, you might sell the most tickets to a band concert or other event and by doing so, win a free camping trip or some sports equipment. Or, as a reward for washing the dishes all week, you could be taken to a carnival by your parents.

Some income is not earned. A young person often receives an allowance without working for it. Many people receive gifts of money at birthdays or on other special occasions.

Whatever the source of money income, no one person uses this income exactly like another. You

Some children might like to use part of their income to buy a puppy; others might buy comic books or candy.

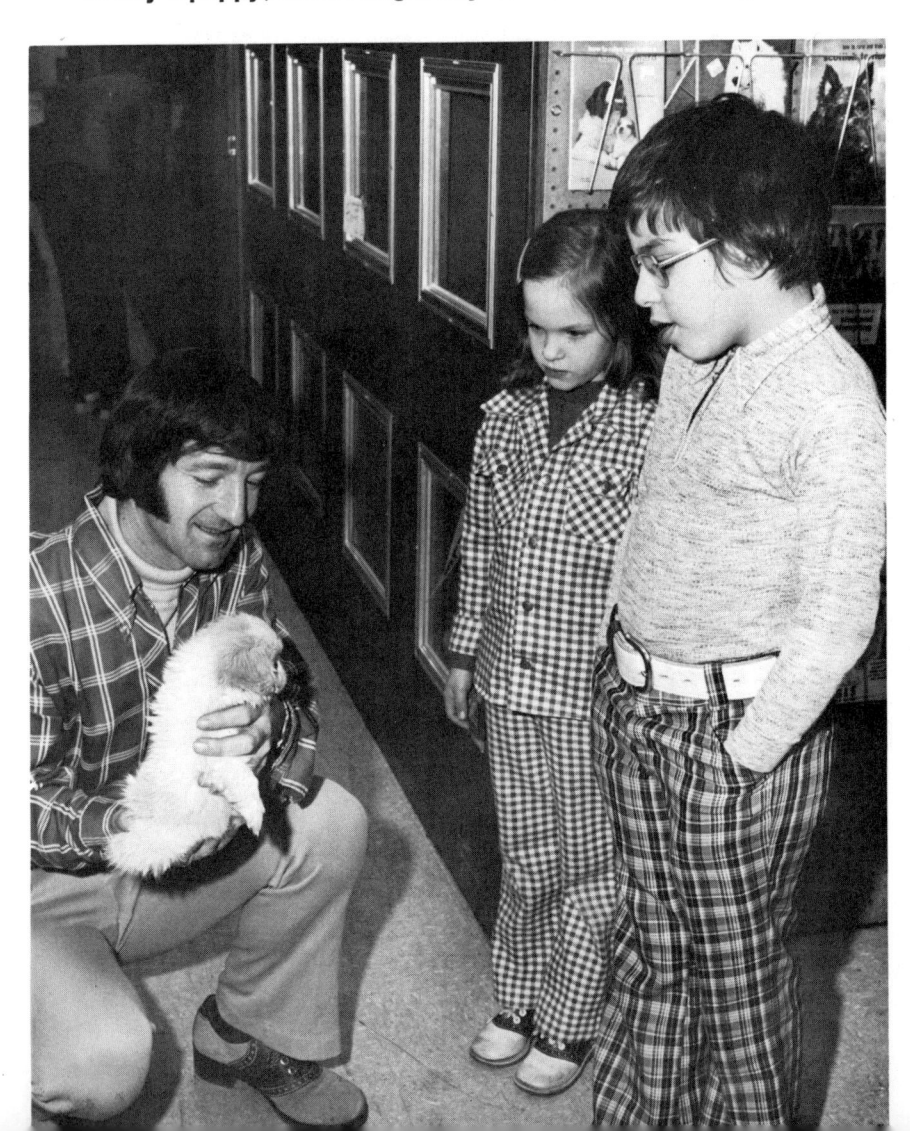

might save part of yours; another person might spend all of it. How you use your income depends on what you value and think is important. If your hobby is photography, you might buy a camera. Or you might buy a ticket to a movie or ball game. Another person might buy a pair of socks, a hat, or some other clothing he or she needs.

Maybe you give part of your income to a church or temple or to charity. You might spend some of your income on toys and candy or comic books and models. Maybe you use most of your income for guitar lessons, or to learn judo or skiing.

During your lifetime, you will have to make many decisions as a consumer. At first, the choices will seem very simple. But as you get older, your income will increase and your responsibilities and values will change. Choices will become more complex.

As an adult consumer, you might have to make choices that range from whether to save for a vacation to everyday decisions such as what foods to buy for your family. You might have to decide whether you should buy a washing machine, or take your clothes to a laundromat to be washed instead. Should you buy a big, fancy, used car, or a small, economy-sized, new car? Should you pay rent for a house or apartment, or should you buy a home of your own?

The variety of choices seems endless. But whatever decisions you make—now or in the future—many of those decisions will depend on what goods and services are available and where you buy them in the marketplace.

For now, you may have to choose which soft drink to buy.

right here
Dr Pepper
SUGAR FREE
Diet Rite
CLUB SODA
Teem
PEPSI
DIET PEPSI

CHAPTER TWO

WHERE YOU CAN BUY

A *marketplace* can be booths and stalls in a large outdoor area where people sell homegrown or handmade goods. It can be a few neighborhood stores. It can be hundreds of different stores in a downtown section of a big city. It can be dozens of businesses in a mall or shopping center which serves several towns.

Whatever the size of the marketplace in your area, it is where you go to buy goods and services. And you probably have a choice in the types of stores and businesses in which you can shop.

For food, your family might go to a supermarket, delicatessen, or corner grocery. Maybe you some-

A catalog is a type of marketplace for many people who cannot easily get to stores and shops to buy.

Many people like to shop in neighborhood stores—such as this drugstore—because the stores provide "friendly service" and convenience; they are familiar places and within walking distance of the people living nearby.

A shopping center, with many different types of stores, is a popular marketplace for people who live in suburbs.

times go to a restaurant to eat. Or perhaps you occasionally get sandwiches, drinks, or candy from a vending machine. There are shops where you can get your hair cut or styled. Your family probably goes to a fix-it shop to get repair services for a radio, TV, or vacuum cleaner. Maybe you take your clothes to a dry cleaning store, go along with your parents to a furniture store, a hardware store, or a gas station.

Where you decide to shop in the marketplace depends, of course, on what you need or want. But there are other things to think about, too. Where you buy could be determined by how close you live to stores and shops, as well as by the prices you have to pay for goods and services.

In order to shop wisely, you should compare. Learn which stores or businesses you should buy from, and which ones you should avoid. Sometimes just watching and listening will help you decide. Much information about the marketplace is spread by word-of-mouth; people compare by telling each other about the way different stores and businesses operate.

You can also learn what stores have to offer and make comparisons by reading magazines and newspapers. Suppose you are going to shop for groceries for the family. You should check the different grocery store ads in your local newspaper. Or you might read the printed grocery ads that come through the mail or are handed out.

Maybe the Conway Store is running an ad offering two pounds of bananas for thirty-nine cents, or twenty cents a pound. The Big Value Store is selling bananas for fifteen cents a pound, and also advertises lower prices for some meats and canned goods your family needs. If you shopped at the Big Value Store, you could save some money. So, this would be a good place to buy the family groceries.

Some choices in the marketplace could depend on how urgently you need something. What if you have an upset stomach one night, and there is nothing in the house to soothe it? Your father could get medication at a discount drugstore where prices are low. However, that store is all the way across town. There is a neighborhood drugstore just around the corner. And, even though it costs more for the medication at the corner store, it is worth it. Time, which is important in this case, was saved by shopping in the neighborhood store.

People buy many types of services in the marketplace. The services of a dependable mechanic for auto repairs is just one example.

Other considerations which help determine where to buy are honesty, promptness, and courtesy. For example, who wants to hire a repairman if he doesn't fix things properly, or if he pretends he's done extra work in order to increase his bill? And who likes to go to a restaurant where meals are served by waiters or waitresses who are slow and unpleasant? Whatever the service you pay for, if it is poor, unfair, or dishonest, you should make a complaint. Workers or business owners often provide better service when they know a customer is dissatisfied and is going to go elsewhere.

For some services you need, there is little or no choice in the marketplace. Almost everyone uses electric, gas, telephone, transportation, and water services. But consumers cannot go to several different electric companies, say, to determine which one will serve them better and charge the lowest *rate* (money paid for the service).

Such a service is provided by one company called a public utility. It serves nearly everyone in a city, state or large area. The company has a "natural monopoly." That is, it is allowed by the federal government to operate without competition. However, a public utility company is regulated by federal and state laws which set health and safety standards and rates. A public utility company that provides power (gas or electricity) for example, can only charge rates set by the state power commission. If consumers feel rates are unfair, they should complain to their local public utility company and to their state power commission.

Public schools, public libraries, fire and police protection, garbage collection, street and highway repairs, are examples of the services that are provided by local and state governments. Consumers do not "shop" for these services, either. They are paid for through taxes. People depend on officials, who are elected or appointed, to see that these services are

ARROW
SH
Manhattan SHIR
CONED
IS ROBBING US!
WE'RE FIGHTING MAD!
Women United for Action

Although you have no
choice as to where you buy
gas and electric power,
you as a consumer can
take action.
Here consumers picket a meeting
held by Con Ed in New York City.
Earlier this year (1974) consumers
who owned all-electric homes
protested high rates to the
Public Service Commission.

(Wide World Photos)

provided. If consumers are dissatisfied and want changes in government services, they need to make complaints to government officials. Citizens can also voice their dissatisfaction by voting into office people who will bring about the changes they want in services.

Except for the government and public utility services, you and your family have many choices in the marketplace. And sometimes it can be difficult to decide where to shop. Through advertising, businesses compete to get your attention so you will buy from their stores or companies. Most ads try to show that a certain product or service is what consumers need and want, and is the best they can buy. Such advertising can have an effect on your buying decisions. But you can guard against being taken in by advertising, if you understand why you buy.

CHAPTER THREE

WHY YOU BUY

You bought lunch in the school cafeteria because you were hungry. A friend broke his leg, and his parents paid a doctor for the medical services he needed. The man next door bought a raincoat so he wouldn't get wet in the rain.

These reasons for buying are clear. All people must have certain goods and services for survival or protection. But there are other reasons that *motivate* you, or make you decide to buy. These motivations are not as clear-cut as the others. They are based on wants or wishes, not on needs.

For example, most people want to be like their friends and be part of the group. They also like to have fun. These wants motivate many consumers to buy certain types of products.

Let's say there is an imaginary product called Marvel Mounts. It's a type of shoe to which you can attach rollers, gliders, or springs. With these Marvel Mounts, you can bounce, hop, slide, roll, or glide wherever you want to go!

Several of your friends have the Marvel Mounts, but you don't. So you begin to feel left out.

"All the other kids have Marvel Mounts," you say. "Why can't I? I need a pair, too!"

You might feel you really need the shoes. But if you buy such a product, you are probably being motivated by a desire to be like everybody else, as well as to have fun.

There are also many people who want to attract attention and feel important. This could motivate them to buy such things as flashy jewelry, fancy ice skates, or racy sports cars. They don't need any of these things to survive. But such products often stand out as being "better," or different from what their friends or relatives have. This could make the others sit up and take notice.

Many times people buy products because they want to enter contests that are described on the packages, or because they want the "gifts" inside. Breakfast cereal packages often have such appeals; they attract the attention of children who urge their parents to buy the products. The costs for the prizes and gifts are usually added to the prices charged for the goods.

Coupon offers attached to products or on packages are used to motivate people to buy. You can sometimes save money if coupons can be used to collect refunds or to get a discount (several cents off). However, the refund or discount means little if the product is not what you want, is higher priced than others of the same quality, or if you must spend money for mailing costs to collect the refund.

The desire to be accepted by other people, or to stand out from the crowd are not the only reasons people buy. Have you ever gone to a drive-in restaurant to get a paper hat, a toy, or game that is offered "free" with a hamburger order? Maybe you bought a product so you could enter a contest (using the entry blank on the package) with the hope that you would win a prize. Or perhaps you persuaded your mother to buy a certain cereal that had a game, car, ring, or other "gift" inside the package or attached to it.

Many people buy because they hope to get something for nothing. In fact, people often buy a package for the prize rather than the product inside. However, the cost of the prize or gift is usually added to the price charged for the product. Manufacturers and advertisers use these gimmicks to motivate consumers.

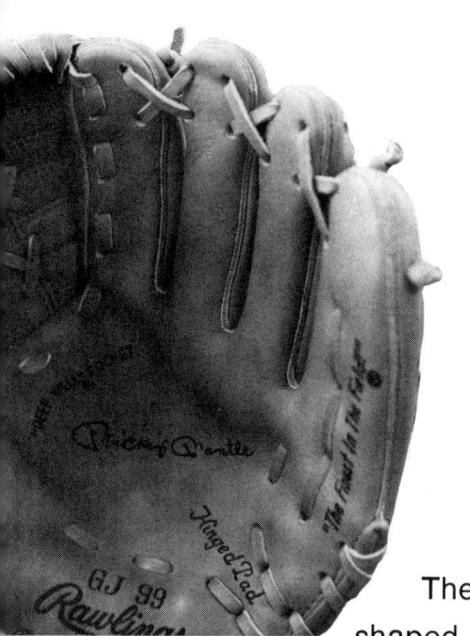

If a person wants to identify with a famous individual, he might buy a product that carries the name of a well-known personality, such as this Mickey Mantle baseball glove.

The way certain packages and containers are shaped also motivate buyers. For instance, you might see a container that looks like an oversized tooth. Inside are small pieces of bubble gum. You could probably buy several times the amount of gum in plain wrappers for the same price you pay for gum in the special container. So, if you buy, is it because you *really* want the gum, or because you want the big tooth container?

Not only packages, but products, too, are often designed to attract buyers. Balloons, vitamins, even electric toothbrushes are shaped like cartoon characters. Pads of paper are made to look like apples or cans of soup or almost anything that would catch the attention of consumers—and increase sales.

Some people want to identify with famous individuals. So they buy products such as shoes, shirts, jackets, and sports equipment that carry the names of well-known personalities. Suppose you want a base-

Cartoon characters, such as Charlie Brown and Snoopy, are often used to promote products. Children buy such items because the cartoon characters are popular and likable; thus it seems the products too should be likable.

ball bat. Several kinds of bats would be good to use when you play with a neighborhood team. But a Hank Aaron bat might seem "the best" simply because it's stamped with his name. You could pretend you were just like Hank Aaron when you used the bat.

Most of us want to look good and have good feelings about ourselves. This could motivate us to buy such things as lotions, shampoo, and stylish clothes.

29

Through advertising, the "golden arches" of a restaurant chain have become well-known across the country. The arches identify the restaurant and are a means for attracting customers. These symbols are easily recognized, and people often buy because a place or product is familiar to them.

The reasons why people buy are endless. And advertisers know that people are motivated to buy to satisfy their wants or wishes. So they often create ads that suggest a person will be popular, have fun, be important, be like famous people, or just feel good—*if* he or she uses a particular product or service.

No one has to give in to such advertising messages. We are all free to make choices. The more we can understand our own needs and what we want and can afford, the easier it is to make our choices on the basis of what is best for us.

CHAPTER FOUR

BEWARE OF BALLYHOO!

"New, Low Prices! Buy Now!"

"Munchy Marshmallow Melts. Get the Fun Size!"

"Try New, Improved Bilbos! Packed with Nutrition!"

These are the kinds of advertisements you probably hear or read every day. You might also see ads on TV which claim a product, such as a toy car, is "like

Newspapers often carry ads for sales or discount items in stores. The ads are designed to motivate people to buy in certain places of business.

the real thing." Or maybe you hear a radio commercial for bread that "builds strong bodies."

Then there is the type of ad that claims **Prices Slashed!** or **Storewide Sale** or **Gigantic Savings!** Or maybe a store advertises "specials" or "discounts." Such offers suggest that a certain amount of money has been subtracted from the regular prices.

Many stores advertise "specials" in order to get customers to come inside to buy.

Some of these advertising claims are true. Others, however, are ballyhoo. In order to attract customers, they stretch the truth. So how do you determine which ads are false and which ones honestly represent the facts?

You can begin by looking into sales and discount offers. Sometimes stores display goods that are **On Sale** but are of lower quality than what the store usually sells. For example, a clothing store might always carry shirts that are the latest style and made of material that wears a long time. These shirts might sell for ten or fifteen dollars. However, when the owner decides to have a sale, he orders plain shirts made of cheaper material. They are advertised as **Special Purchase: Shirts on Sale—$5.00.** Customers come to buy, and many believe they are getting the kind of shirts always sold in the store.

Sometimes price tags on merchandise are marked **25% Off** or **50% Off.** But first, the regular prices were marked up. For instance, certain slacks might normally sell for around ten dollars a pair, but a tag has been made up to show the slacks once sold for twenty dollars. Then if customers buy the "twenty dollar" slacks for fifty percent off, they pay what the slacks cost when not on sale.

You can avoid being tricked by such gimmicks if you know how much items usually cost, and if you compare prices of similar merchandise in different stores whenever you shop.

33

A "2-for-1" sale (two items for the price of one) is a good way to save money—*if* you need the items you buy on sale.

Even when sales are honest, you should still be on the alert. Don't buy just because a sale is going on, or because you happen to see discount items and have a sudden urge to buy. Maybe there's a **1¢ Sale** in a drugstore. You can buy one toothbrush for eighty-nine cents and another for just one cent more. If you already have an extra toothbrush, it could be wasteful to buy two more just because you can get them on sale. On the other hand, if you need a toothbrush, you are really saving money if you take advantage of the one cent sale.

So look for sales when you buy, but beware of any sale item you don't need. No matter what the price, it can be worthless to you if you have no use for it.

When it comes to advertising claims for individual products, how can you determine whether these are true or false? The best way is to test or experiment with the products yourself. Don't just accept as fact the experiments you see on TV.

Another way to test products is by tasting. Compare various brands of a similar product. Find out, for example, whether a brand of peanut butter is "creamy smooth" as the label claims, and which brand tastes the best to you. *Your preference—* **what you like—should determine what you buy, not the claims of advertisers.**

For example, take paper towels. If ads show that certain paper towels "absorb better," try out several brands. Use a water or grease test. See which towel soaks up the best and whether you have to use fewer towels of one brand to do the cleanup job. Also, if an ad claims a towel is "softer," determine whether you think softness has anything to do with the way the towel is used. Finally, you might ask yourself: do I really need the paper towels at all? Could I use cloth towels or sponges instead? Those could be re-used many times and would not add to pollution problems.

Listen to words used to advertise products like cleaning powders. Do words such as "foamy" and "white tornado" suggest products will work better? Test whether such characteristics as foam and suds make a difference in the way a product cleans. Scrub a tub or sink with several different brands. Does any one cleaner clean better than another?

In TV ads for dry breakfast cereals and snack foods (potato chips, pizzas, etc.), the products are usually associated with lively people or bouncy cartoon characters. This often gives the impression that the foods are energy producing or nutritious. Have a parent, teacher, or school nurse help you determine whether that is true. With their help, you can check facts on nutrition and food value in science books and health magazines.

Some claims for toys can be checked out by doing

a simple survey. Jot down a description of some toys you see advertised on television, along with the claims made for each. Then, take those descriptions to a toy store or department store and see if they match the actual products on display. Are the toys the size they seemed to be on TV? Do you have to buy any extras such as batteries, plastic parts or paint?

There is often a good deal of ballyhoo in advertising claims for toys. One thing to check when buying products like models and racing sets is how many "extra" items you'll need to buy in order to enjoy the product.

Also, check with friends or relatives who may have purchased some of the toys on your survey sheet. Let them tell you how they would rate the advertising claims. Exaggerated? Partly true? All true?

You can take surveys by mail, too. Make up questionnaires, based on advertising claims, to send manufacturing companies. Ask each company how it determines the effectiveness of its product. What tests are used, for example, to prove that a toothpaste prevents cavities? Then check any information you receive with your dentist. Find out if it's necessary to whiten teeth? Does the toothpaste abrasive, which shines the teeth, do any damage to the tooth enamel? What are the basic ingredients of different toothpastes? Are they the same or similar for each brand? If so, does it matter which toothpaste you buy?

In short, ask questions about any advertising claims. Don't believe all that you see and hear. There is a centuries-old Latin phrase which still applies today: *caveat emptor* — "Let the buyer beware!" With that thought as your guide, make your own comparisons. Then you will be able to find out which advertising claims are true and which are not.

CHAPTER FIVE

WHAT'S THE BEST BUY?

A used car sits on a lot with a sign **Best Buy. Beat This Low Price. $1,500.** In a discount store a sign says **Best Buys in Town. Portable TVs $50.** In a variety store a bin with a mixture of such items as packages of notebook paper, felt pens, and boxes of colored pencils is labeled **Best Buys 29¢.**

From signs like these, you could get the idea that any product with a low price is a good buy or the best buy. However, *quality* (how well a product is made) and *durability* (how long it will last) should be checked, too.

How a product is made and what material is used might determine whether it's a good buy. Here, a bat made of wood is compared with one of aluminum. The best buy could depend on which lasts the longest or which hits the best.

Maybe you want a jigsaw puzzle. You see one for eighty-nine cents and another for seventy-nine cents. The higher-priced puzzle is made of heavy cardboard; the other is made of very thin cardboard. Both have the kind of picture you like. Which would be the best buy?

If you just wanted to put the puzzle together once, the cheaper one would be the best buy. But if you like to work a puzzle over and over again, the heavier, more expensive one would hold up better and therefore be the best buy.

You should also check quality and durability when you are buying such products as furniture and clothing. But another factor could enter in, too—*maintenance,* or the care that will be needed. If you have the choice, for example, between two jackets which are the same price, but one can be washed and one must be drycleaned, which is the best buy? To dryclean a jacket often costs over two dollars each time. But washing it in a laundromat or at home in a washer usually costs less than fifty cents. So the washable jacket is the better buy.

When you are comparing food products to find the best buy, you should check the different-sized pack-

Tags on clothing give instructions for cleaning or washing, and can help you decide whether a garment will be expensive to keep clean.

To find the best buy in food products, you should check the *unit price*. For example, the price for a quart of milk might be 37¢. A half gallon of the same brand might sell for 64¢. Since there are two quarts in a half gallon, the unit price for the half gallon is 32¢ per quart. Thus, the best buy is the half gallon of milk.

ages. Candy bars are just one type of product sold in packs. For example, one package containing five bars sells for forty-nine cents; another pack with ten bars sells for eighty-nine cents. To find out which pack is the best buy, you need to know the *unit price,* or the cost of one candy bar in each of the two different packs. Divide the price of each pack by the number of bars in it. The bars in the forty-nine cent pack cost almost ten cents apiece, while the bars in the eighty-nine cent pack cost about nine cents apiece. So the larger pack is the best buy.

You should also compare the weights of packaged foods and liquids. Suppose you've invited nine friends to your birthday party, and you want to buy enough pretzels. A store is selling separate packages of one-and-one-half ounces each for fifteen cents apiece. There are also large **Economy** packages of ten ounces each for forty-nine cents. So which would you buy?

If you want to get the most for your money, you would buy two large **Economy** packages for a total of twenty ounces at ninety-eight cents. The cost of ten smaller packages, weighing a total of fifteen ounces, would be one dollar and fifty cents.

Yet, you do not always get the best buy just because a product is packaged in the **Economy Size, Family Size, Giant Size,** or **Jumbo Size.** The words are often used on packages to attract buyers who

Sometimes a product packaged in a large container (box A) can be a better buy than that same product packaged in a smaller size container (box B). But you have to check the weight in each package, along with price, to find the unit cost, or the amount charged for each ounce.

Fruit drinks often seem like a good buy because you get a large quantity at a price less than you would pay for the same amount of fruit juice. But fruit juice and fruit drink are not the same. A juice squeezed from fruit and frozen or bottled is usually more nutritious than a drink that has only a small portion of juice and is mostly water, sugar and flavoring. Check the labels of such products to make sure.

hope to save money. In some instances, the unit price is less on the smaller package. Often, the unit price on each size package is the same, or it only differs by a fraction of a cent. Again, you can find out by dividing the price of a package by the amount of items or number of ounces listed on the label. There is this to consider, too. If you are buying food and cannot use all that's in a large size, the better buy would be the smaller size, since there won't be leftovers which might be wasted.

Ingredients on labels should be compared, too. Federal law requires that contents of food products be

44

This is an example of the way products must be labeled to provide nutrition information as required by federal law.

listed according to the amount and importance of each ingredient. In other words, a label on a can of one brand of chicken noodle soup might list the chicken broth (liquid) first. Noodles might be listed next, then chicken, then spices, and so on. Compare this list with one from another brand of chicken noodle soup. If they are the same, are the prices the same?

Another federal law requires that nutrients such as vitamins, minerals, and protein be listed on labels for all diet foods, as well as for foods which companies claim are "fortified," "enriched," or in some way improve health. Labels for such foods must also show the amount of nutrients in a typical serving (a cup of soup, for example), and the percentage of the Recommended Daily Allowance (RDA) of selected vitamins, minerals, and protein in each serving. The RDA is the standard, set by the Food and Drug Administration, for the amount of nutrients needed by an adult.

Since every person needs vitamins, minerals, and other nutrients for good health, check to see if such ingredients are listed on the food products you buy. Many companies are adding this information to their labels even though they may not be required to do so under this law. A good buy could depend on whether you are getting a nutritious food as opposed to a product with little food value.

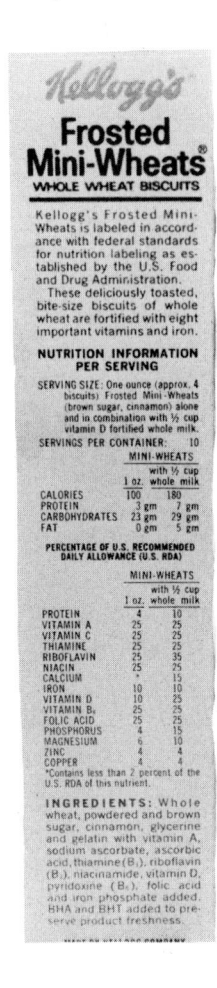

45

One other factor to consider when you're shopping is the *store brand* and how it compares with a *name brand.* Name brands are products that are nationally advertised and known across the country by their trademarks, such as 7-Up, Band Aid, and Scotch Tape. Store brands, on the other hand, are products sold in certain stores only. They have the store label such as "Walgreen" on their drug items and "Ann Page" on A & P products.

Many store brand products such as food, soft drinks, aspirin, soap, plastic bandage strips, and paper tissues are identical or practically the same as name brands. Yet, because of national advertising, people often think of products by name brands. As a result, they ask for products by their trademark — Coke or Kleenex, for example — instead of a cola drink or paper tissue. Many consumers are convinced that a name brand is a better product, simply because they have heard the name or seen the trademark so often. However, most name brands are higher priced than store brands. Manufacturers add the costs of their advertising to the prices of their products.

Look at vitamins. Maybe your mother always buys a name brand multiple vitamin. Compare that product with a multiple vitamin product packaged by a discount, grocery, or drugstore. Make sure you compare *the same size* package. You will probably find that the store brand sells for half the price of the name brand.

Is that because the expensive vitamin is a better product, and thus worth more money? Again, compare. The labels will probably show that the various vitamin and mineral units in each tablet are identical or nearly the same for both brands. So, the best buy would be the product that costs less.

There is a general formula you can use to measure whether the goods or services you buy are worth

Often store brand products sell for less than name brands. This is because advertising costs of the name brands are added to the prices of the goods.

A simple hand calculator can help you keep track of purchases. If you add up items as you go, you won't spend more than you had intended.

the money you pay, or if they are the best buy for your money.

1. Determine what you need and want.
2. Ask yourself: How are you going to use the product?
3. Check similar types of products.
4. Compare the price and quality.
5. Select the best buy.

CHAPTER SIX

HOW IS A CONSUMER PROTECTED?

REPORTER FINDS HOT DOG "SPIKED."

This headline recently appeared in a Midwestern newspaper. In the article, the reporter described her experience with a frankfurter. She had prepared it for lunch, and as she was biting into it, she noticed what looked like a hard, black seed. She poked at the object and found it was the head of a "spike," a sharp two-inch nail. What if the nail had caught in her throat?

The reporter had had a close call. She decided to write a story about her experience. In it, she would describe her search to find out whether consumers are protected from such hazards in the marketplace.

First, the reporter went back to the store where she bought the package of hot dogs, and complained to the store manager. He began making inquiries at the meat-packing plant that processed the hot dogs.

The U.S. Department of Agriculture uses this type of stamp to indicate that beef has been inspected and graded for quality. This should be a form of protection for consumers. However, such stamps are seldom visible after meat is trimmed and packaged for sale.

The next step was to call an office of the United States Department of Agriculture (USDA). This federal agency, with headquarters in Washington, D.C., has regional and state offices around the country. One of its functions is to inspect meat and poultry-packing plants for cleanliness. Inspectors also look for spoiled meat, and they check to see if poultry, eggs, and egg products are fresh.

In the case of the "spiked" hot dog, the inspector found no unsanitary conditions in the meat-packing plant. However, he did turn up evidence that suggested the nail had been forced into the hot dog after processing, probably by a dissatisfied worker.

Only one vicious trick of this type was uncovered, but the story points up the need for consumers to act. Had there been problems with debris and filth in the meat, the inspector could have ordered the plant closed. And because one consumer did speak up, thousands of consumers would have been protected from unclean and dangerous food.

Besides the USDA, other federal departments and agencies protect consumers. The Food and Drug Administration (FDA) is one. Part of the U.S. Department of Health, Education and Welfare, the FDA is responsible for enforcing the Food, Drug and Cosmetic Act of 1938. This act requires that foods, drugs, and cosmetics be produced under sanitary conditions and be proven safe for consumers. The act also provides for truthful and informative labeling on foods, as well as warnings on drugs or other products to prevent dangers to health or safety.

For example, the FDA enforces the regulation for labeling nutrients on some food products (as described in the previous chapter). However, millions of Americans, who have health problems such as diabetes and allergies, must know the contents of food products in order to avoid those ingredients or foods which their bodies cannot tolerate and could cause illness or even death. Because of pressure from consumer groups and individuals, Congress is working on

Federal law requires that products with poisonous substances must have labels warning consumers of danger to their health.

legislation that will require *all* ingredients used in food products be listed on labels.

Another act enforced by the FDA is the Toy Safety Act which bans such toys as stoves that can burn young children or mechanical toys with sharp points—these can no longer be manufactured. The FDA also enforces the Hazardous Substances Act. This Act requires that poisonous household products and certain medicines, such as children's aspirin, be packaged in containers that young children cannot open easily. Products which contain poisonous chemicals, such as oven cleaners, must have "Caution," "Danger," or some other word to signal that there is a hazard. The label must also give instructions for emergency care in case the product is swallowed, gets in a person's eyes, or on the skin.

The Federal Trade Commission (FTC) is another federal agency that provides protective services for consumers. Its job is to prevent misleading advertising, price-fixing, and dishonest packaging and selling. This agency has also enforced the ban on cigarette advertising on TV. And it requires the following warning on printed ads in magazines, newspapers and on cigarette packages: "Warning: The Surgeon General Has Determined That Cigarette Smoking is Dangerous To Your Health."

The FTC also enforces laws which prevent the sale of dangerously flammable clothing, such as children's sleepwear, that might catch fire easily. It requires "truth in labeling" fabrics, furs, and furniture. Clothing labels, for example, must tell exactly what

Labels must now be sewn in all clothing to show fabric content. Often these labels are in the neckline or in a seam. This federal law protects consumers by providing information needed to determine care of clothing.

fabrics the garments are made of, such as 100% wool, or 60% cotton and 40% polyester. Labels on garments made of fur must show whether they are man-made or natural. If natural, the labels must tell what animal the fur comes from, and whether the fur is dyed or bleached. With such information, consumers can determine how to care for clothing as well as avoid any fabric, fur or dyed materials to which they might be allergic. Furniture must also have tags that describe the various materials used in their construction. A chair could be made of oak wood, say, or just be finished to look like oak; it could have a seat of leather or "simulated" (imitation) leather. Tags must tell consumers what they are actually buying—natural or artificial materials.

The National Office of Consumer Affairs, which is a federal agency, as well as state and local government agencies for consumer affairs can provide some protection for consumers, too. The state consumer agency is usually in the office of the Attorney General. This office has the legal power to take cases to court to try to correct consumer problems. Except for New York City, local consumer agencies seldom have this legal power. All they can do is advise where to get help if court action is needed. They can also warn consumers about dishonest pricing and other fraud in the marketplace.

Information about a variety of products in the marketplace and other articles of interest to consumers are published in government bulletins, booklets and memos. Many of them are available in public libraries.

You can find addresses for local and state consumer agencies in the telephone directory and also in such directories as the annual *Consumer Action Guide* at your public library. City and state government officials might also be able to guide you to the consumer agency which can be of most help.

In addition there are several types of private consumer-protection agencies. One is a group of industrial and trade associations. Each association sets standards of quality and safety for products manufactured by member companies. If the products meet their standards, they are stamped with "seals of approval." For example, the Underwriters Laboratories (UL) is an agency that sets standards for electrical appliances.

These two magazines of private organizations report to consumers about various types of products and services and how to spend money wisely in the marketplace.

When the agency approves the safety of an iron, toaster, or similar electrical appliance, then the UL seal is stamped on the product. In this way, consumers are guaranteed that the product has been tested for safety.

The Consumers Union is a private organization that protects consumers through its own research. The organization tests and rates the quality of various products and reports on them in its monthly magazine, *Consumer Reports.* It also reports on new laws and brings dishonest practices to the attention of consumers.

The Center for the Study of Responsive Law is a private group that investigates consumer complaints. It was founded in 1969 by Ralph Nader, who has become one of the most publicized "watch dogs" for consumers. Nader, who is a lawyer, first investigated defects of automobiles manufactured by General Motors, Ford, and other large corporations. In 1965, he wrote *Unsafe at any Speed,* a book which attacked the entire automotive industry for its failure to build safe cars. His work helped bring about the National Traffic and Motor Vehicle Safety Act of 1966.

Nader, and the young lawyers and law students assisting him, also worked to get gas companies to install safer pipelines. They have investigated many other industries, and alerted consumers to corrupt or negligent business practices.

The Nader group, often called "Nader's Raiders," has specifically studied governmental agencies such as the FDA and FTC which were set up to protect consumers. A Center report pointed out that these agencies had done little over the years to protect citizens and that the agencies have not strongly enforced laws. Instead, the report continued, they often favored the industries they were supposed to govern and regulate.

The cases brought to court by the Nader group and the influence of other consumer groups have forced some changes, however. Through their efforts,

Congress is now working on a bill to establish a Consumer Protection Agency. One of its functions would be to collect information about goods and services from other government bureaus and publicize consumer problems and complaints. This new agency would also speak for the consumer when such regulatory agencies as the FTC and FDA form policies or new laws. The agency would not be able to make regulations of its own. But it would be able to force government and industry to be more responsive to consumers. As a result, the public would be protected from unsafe and unjust practices in the marketplace.

Perhaps there is a Better Business Bureau (BBB) in your town or city. That organization also provides some help with consumer problems. One of its main functions is to answer questions about local busi-

This is a symbol of the Better Business Bureau, an organization that has offices in many towns and cities. The BBB can provide consumers with information about local businesses.

You can protect yourself in the marketplace by asking questions and carefully inspecting products you plan to buy. For example, before buying a bicycle, you can ask the owner or clerk in the store to explain the various parts, how the bike operates, what you need to do about maintenance, and whether or not there is a guarantee to repair parts if they break or wear out through no fault of your own.

nesses. Before you buy, you can find out whether a company has a record of fair business practices, how long it has been in business, and how it treats customers.

Another way to protect yourself from problems before they develop is to find out whether a product or service you buy comes with a *guarantee* or *warranty*. This is a written promise that a business owner or manufacturer will stand by his products—that certain repairs will be made and faulty parts replaced without charge, or for only a portion of the repair or replacement cost. However, a guarantee or warranty is only as good as the company or business that gives it. If a business is known for not keeping promises, then the guarantee is of little value. Often, though, you can get repairs or have faulty products replaced by returning them to the store where you bought them. In fact, many stores have special departments for adjustments or customer complaints.

You and your family can also write directly to a manufacturer if you are not satisfied with a product. You can also let a company know when you are pleased with a product or have received good services. Such positive action might help convince companies to continue practices which benefit consumers. If you plan to write to companies, you can find addresses on labels and in the *Consumer Action Guide*. Or you can ask a librarian to help you find addresses.

If you have a complaint that is not corrected through the ways already mentioned, then write to a newspaper "action line" or call a local radio or TV program that publicizes consumer problems. Businesses often take action as a result of bad publicity

It is often helpful to write to a newspaper "action line," if you don't get results on your own.

in newspapers or on the air. They don't want a reputation for dishonesty, shoddy service, or selling poor quality goods. This only drives customers away.

Finally, be a *responsible consumer*. That is, be aware of actions any consumer can take to prevent or correct problems in the marketplace. Here is an action guide you can use:

1. Be a comparison shopper.
2. Guard against advertising gimmicks and pro-

motional pressures to buy goods and services you might not want or need.
3. Speak up. Write, call, or talk face-to-face with local business people about faulty goods or unfair practices.
4. Write to companies when you don't get what you pay for.
5. Join local consumer clubs, attend meetings on consumer protection, and read current books and articles on consumerism.
6. Expose dishonest businesses by complaining to government agencies.
7. Write to federal and state legislators about your concerns in the marketplace.
8. Be aware of how you can protect not only yourself as a consumer, but also the environment which is often polluted by certain products.

INDEX

advertisements, 18, 24, 27, 28, 30, 31-33, 35-38, 53, 61
allowance, 12
approval, seals of, 55-56
automotive industry, 57

Better Business Bureau (BBB), 58
brand names, 46-47
business, 16, 18, 20, 32-33, 58-59, 60, 62

Center for the Study of Responsive Law, 57
citizen control, 21, 24
clothing, 9, 13, 25, 28, 33, 41
comparison shopping, 18, 33, 41-43, 48, 61
competition, 21
consumer, 9, 14, 16-18, 19, 21, 24, 27, 28, 60, 61; agencies, 50, 51, 52, 54-58; complaints by, 24, 49-55, 60-62; education of, 38, 59, 62; protection of, 21, 44-45, 49, 51-62; responsibility of, 61-62
Consumer Action Guide, 55, 60
Consumer Protection Agency, 58
Consumer Reports, 56
Consumers Union, 56
Congress, United States, 51-52, 58
convenience, 10, 18, 19

durability, 39-41

Federal Trade Commission (FTC), 52-53, 57, 58
food, 9, 14, 16, 17, 18, 19, 25, 36, 42-43, 44-45, 49-51
Food and Drug Administration (FDA), 45, 51-52, 57, 58
Food, Drug and Cosmetic Act of 1938, 51
food inspection, 50

goods, 9, 10, 11, 13, 14, 16, 28-29, 30, 34, 36-38, 39-41, 57, 58, 62
guarantee (warranty), 60

Hazardous Substances Act, 52

income, 11-14
ingredients, 44-45, 51, 52, 54

jobs, 10, 11

labelling, 45, 46, 51, 52; "truth in," 53-54
laws, 21, 44-45, 51-54, 57, 58
luxuries, 10, 11

maintenance, 41
marketplace, 16, 18, 24, 49, 58, 62
motivation, 25-30

63

Nader, Ralph, 57
"Nader's Raiders," 57
National Office of Consumers Affairs, 54
National Traffic and Motor Vehicle Safety Act of 1966, 57
necessities, 10

packaging, 28, 41-45, 52
pollution, 36, 62
prices, 18-19, 28, 31-34, 39, 40-43
pricing, unit, 42-44
product enhancement, 28-29, 31
product testing, 35-38
publicity, 60-61

quality, 39, 41, 61-62

Recommended Daily Allowance (RDA), 45
religion, 9, 14

sales, 31-34
saving, 13
services, 9, 10, 14, 16, 18, 20, 21, 25, 30, 58, 60; government, 24, 58; public utility, 21, 24, 58, 62
shelter, 9, 14
surveys, 37-38

Toy Safety Law, 52

Underwriters Laboratories (UL), 55, 56
United States Department of Agriculture (USDA), 50
Unsafe at any Speed, 57

values, 13-14, 18, 19, 20, 60

weight, 43